Dedication

To all those who ever struggled with learning a foreign language and to Wolfgang Karfunkel

Also by Yatir Nitzany

Conversational Spanish Quick and Easy

Conversational French Quick and Easy

Conversational Italian Quick and Easy

Conversational Portuguese Quick and Easy

Conversational German Quick and Easy

Conversational Dutch Quick and Easy

Conversational Norwegian Quick and Easy

Conversational Danish Quick and Easy

Conversational Russian Quick and Easy

Conversational Ukrainian Quick and Easy

Conversational Bulgarian Quick and Easy

Conversational Polish Quick and Easy

Conversational Hebrew Quick and Easy

Conversational Yiddish Quick and Easy

Conversational Armenian Quick and Easy

Conversational Arabic Quick and Easy

Conversational Portuguese Quick and Easy
The Most Innovative Technique to Learn the Portuguese Language

Part I

YATIR NITZANY

Translated by:
Gloria Cavallaho Lawerence

Interior Design:
Menachem Otto

Copyright © 2014
Yatir Nitzany
All rights reserved.
ISBN-13: 978-1951244033
Printed in the United States of America

Foreword

About Myself

For many years I struggled to learn Spanish, and I still knew no more than about twenty words. Consequently, I was extremely frustrated. One day I stumbled upon this method as I was playing around with word combinations. Suddenly, I came to the realization that every language has a certain core group of words that are most commonly used and, simply by learning them, one could gain the ability to engage in quick and easy conversational Spanish.

I discovered which words those were, and I narrowed them down to three hundred and fifty that, once memorized, one could connect and create one's own sentences. The variations were and are *infinite*! By using this incredibly simple technique, I could converse at a proficient level and speak Spanish. Within a week, I astonished my Spanish-speaking friends with my newfound ability. The next semester I registered at my university for a Spanish language course, and I applied the same principles I had learned in that class (grammar, additional vocabulary, future and past tense, etc.) to those three hundred and fifty words I already had memorized, and immediately I felt as if I had grown wings and learned how to fly.

At the end of the semester, we took a class trip to San José, Costa Rica. I was like a fish in water, while the rest of my classmates were floundering and still struggling to converse. Throughout the following months, I again applied the same principle to other languages—French, Portuguese, Italian, and Arabic, all of which I now speak proficiently, thanks to this very simple technique.

This method is by far the fastest way to master quick and easy conversational language skills. There is no other technique that compares to my concept. It is effective, it worked for me, and it will work for you. Be consistent with my program, and you too will succeed the way I and many, many others have.

Table of Contents

Introduction to the Program 8

Introduction to the Portuguese to Language 10

Memorization Made Easy...11

Note to the Reader 13

The Program 15

Building Bridges 37

Basic Grammatical Requirements of the Portuguese to Language..........42

Reading and Pronunciation...46

Conclusion..51

Note from the Author 52

Introduction to the Program

People often dream about learning a foreign language, but usually they never do it. Some feel that they just won't be able to do it while others believe that they don't have the time. Whatever your reason is, it's time to set that aside. With my new method, you will have enough time, and you will not fail. You will actually learn how to speak the fundamentals of the language—fluently in as little as a few days. Of course, you won't speak perfect Portuguese to at first, but you will certainly gain significant proficiency. For example, if you travel to Brazil, you will almost effortlessly be able engage in basic conversational communication with the locals in the present tense and you will no longer be intimidated by culture shock. It's time to relax. Learning a language is a valuable skill that connects people of multiple cultures around the world—and you now have the tools to join them.

How does my method work? I have taken twenty-seven of the most commonly used languages in the world and distilled from them the three hundred and fifty most frequently used words in any language. This process took three years of observation and research, and during that time, I determined which words I felt were most important for this method of basic conversational communication. In that time, I chose these words in such a way that they were structurally interrelated and that, when combined, form sentences. Thus, once you succeed in memorizing these words, you will be able to combine these words and form your own sentences. The words are spread over twenty pages. In fact, there are just nine basic words that will effectively build bridges, enabling you to speak in an understandable manner (please see Building Bridges, page 37). The words will also combine easily in sentences, for example, enabling you to ask simple questions, make basic statements, and obtain a rudimentary understanding of others' communications. I have also created Memorization-Made-Easy Techniques (See page 11) for this program in order to help with the memorization of the vocabulary. Please see Reading and Pronounciation (Page 46) in order to gain proficiency in the reading and pronunciation of the Portuguese to language prior to starting this program.

My book is mainly intended for basic present tense vocal communication, meaning anyone can easily use it to "get by" linguistically while visiting a foreign country without learning the entire language. With practice, you will be 100 percent understandable to native speakers, which is your aim. One disclaimer: this is *not* a grammar book, though it does address minute and essential grammar rules (see Basic Grammatical Requirements of the Portuguese to Language, Page 43). Therefore, understanding complex sentences with obscure words in Portuguese to is beyond the scope of this book.

People who have tried this method have been successful, and by the time you finish this book, you will understand and be understood in basic conversational Portuguese to. This is the best basis to learn not only the Portuguese to language but any language. This is an entirely revolutionary, no-fail concept, and your ability to combine the pieces of the "language puzzle" together will come with *great* ease, especially if you use this program prior to beginning a Portuguese to class.

This is the best program that was ever designed to teach the reader how to become conversational. Other conversational programs will only teach you phrases. But this is the *only* program that will teach you how to create your *own* sentences for the purpose of becoming conversational.

The Portuguese to Language

Portuguese has over 200 million native speakers, and it is the sixth most common language in the world. The language originated from Latin roots and became popular after a Roman invasion of the western region of the Iberian Peninsula (the area known today as Portugal) during the third century BC. The incoming Romans blended their language with that of the natives, so Portuguese began to change. Traders of the time began to use the language, so it spread rapidly, making its way into Africa and Asia and eventually Brazil. In fact, before the language was officially modernized, it was quite unique. Today, there are more traces of Greek and Latin and fewer words from the original Portuguese language.

Spoken in: Portugal, Brazil, Angola, Mozambique, Guinea-Bissau, Cape Verde, and São Tomé and Príncipe

Memorization Made Easy

There is no doubt the three hundred and fifty words in my program are the required essentials in order to engage in quick and easy basic conversation in any foreign language. However, some people may experience difficulty in the memorization. For this reason, I created Memorization Made Easy. This memorization technique will make this program so simple and fun that it's unbelievable! I have spread the words over the following twenty pages. Each page contains a vocabulary table of ten to fifteen words. Below every vocabulary box, sentences are composed from the words on the page that you have just studied. This aids greatly in memorization. Once you succeed in memorizing the first page, then proceed to the second page. Upon completion of the second page, go back to the first and review. Then proceed to the third page. After memorizing the third, go back to the first and second and repeat. And so on. As you continue, begin to combine words and create your own sentences in your head. Every time you proceed to the following page, you will notice words from the previous pages will be present in those simple sentences as well, because repetition is one of the most crucial aspects in learning any foreign language. Upon completion of your twenty pages, *congratulations*, you have absorbed the required words and gained a basic, quick-and-easy proficiency and you should now be able to create your own sentences and say anything you wish in the Portuguese to language. This is a crash course in conversational Portuguese to, and it works!

Note to the Reader

The purpose of this book is merely to enable you to communicate in Portuguese to. In the program itself, you may notice that the composition of some of those sentences might sound rather clumsy. This is intentional. These sentences were formulated in a specific way to serve two purposes: to facilitate the easy memorization of the vocabulary *and* to teach you how to combine the words in order to form your own sentences for quick and easy communication, rather than making complete literal sense in the English language. So keep in mind that this is *not* a phrase book!

As the title suggests, the sole purpose of this program is for conversational use *only*. It is based on the mirror translation technique. These sentences, as well as the translations are *not* incorrect, just a little clumsy. Latin languages, Semitic languages, and Anglo-Germanic languages, as well as a few others, are compatible with the mirror translation technique.

Many users say that this method surpasses any other known language learning technique that is currently out there on the market. Just stick with the program and you will achieve wonders!

In order to succeed with my method, please start on the very first page of the program and fully master one page at a time prior to proceeding to the next. Otherwise, you will overwhelm yourself and fail. Please do *not* skip pages, nor start from the middle of the book.

It is a myth that certain people are born with the talent to learn a language, and this book disproves that myth. With this method, anyone can learn a foreign language as long as he or she follows these *explicit* directions:

* Memorize the vocabulary on each page.
* Follow that memorization by using a notecard to cover the words you have just memorized and test yourself.
* Then read the sentences following that are created from the vocabulary bank that you just mastered.
* Once fully memorized, give yourself the green light to proceed to the next page.

Again, if you proceed to the following page without mastering the previous, you are guaranteed to gain nothing from this book. If you follow the prescribed steps, you will realize just how effective and simplistic this method is.

The Program

Let's Begin! "Vocabulary" (Memorize the Vocabulary)

I – Eu / **I am** - Eu sou / Estou
With you - Contigo / **With us** - conosco
With him / with her - Com Ele / Com Ela
He - Ele / **He is** - Ele é (permanent), ele está (temporary)
She – Ela / **She is** - Ela é (permanent), ele está (temporary)
Are you - Você está / Você é
For you - Para você
Without him - Sem ele/**Without them (masculine)** - Sem Eles/**(fem)** Sem elas
This - Isto / **Is** - Está / É
Always - Sempre / **Sometimes** - Algumas Vezes
Was – Estive /**fui**
Maybe - Talvez
Better - Melhor
From - De / Do

Sentences from the vocabulary (now you can speak the sentences and combine the words).

Are you at the house?
Você está em casa?
Sometimes I go without him.
Às vezes eu vou sem ele.
I am always with her
Estou sempre com ela
I am from Manaus
Eu sou **de** Manaus
Are you from Brazil?
Você é do Brasil?
I am with you
Estou contigo
This is for you
Isto e para você
Are you alone today?
Você está sozinho hoje?

Concerning eu sou, estou / é, esta and *você está, você é*, please refer to page #43.

*This *isn't* a phrase book! The purpose of this book is *solely* to provide you with the tools to create *your own* sentences!

You - Você / Tu / (plural) Vocês
Good - (M) Bom / **(F)** boa
I was – Estive **/ fui**
Tomorrow - Amanhã
Yes - Sim
No/ don't/ doesn't - Não
The - O / A / Os / As
Same - Mesmo / Igual
Here - Aqui
It's - Está / É
And - E
Between - Entre
Now - Agora
Later / After - Depois
If - Se
Then - Então
Also / too / as well - Também

I was home at 5pm
Eu estava em casa às 17:00
Between now and tomorrow.
Entre agora e amanhã.
It's better to be home later.
É melhor estar em casa mais tarde.
If this is good, then I am happy.
Se isso é bom, então eu estou feliz.
Yes, you are very good
Sim, você e muito bom
I was here with them
Eu estive aqui com eles
You and I
Você e eu
The same day
O mesmo dia

*Concerning *estar, ser*, please refer to page #43.

*Concerning *o, as, os* and *as*, please see page #42.

Me - Me / mim
Where - Onde
Somewhere - Algum lugar
There - Lá / Ali
Ok - Ok
Even if - Inclusive
Afterwards - Depois
Worse - Pior
Everything - Tudo
What - Que
Almost - Quase

Afterwards is worse
Depois é pior
Even if I go now
Inclusive eu vou agora
Where is everything?
Onde está tudo?
Maybe somewhere
Talvez em algum lugar
What? I am almost there
Que? Estou quase lá
Where are you?
Onde está você?
This is for us.
Isto é para nós.
Where is the airport
Onde é o aeroporto.

House - Casa
Home – Lar
Car - Auto / Carro
Son - Filho
Daughter - Filha
Without us - Sem nós
Hello - Alô / Olá / Oi
Good morning - Bom dia
How are you? - Como está você?
Where are you from? - De onde você é
What is your name? - Qual é o seu nome?
How old are you? - Quantos anos você tem?
Hard - Difícil / Duro
Today - Hoje
At - Em / (M)No / (F)Na
Very - Muito
In - Em / Dentro
Already - Já

She is without a car, so maybe she is still at the house?
Ela está sem um carro, talvez ela está ainda em casa
I am in the car already with your son and daughter
Eu já estou no carro com teu filho e filha
Good morning, how are you today?
Bom dia, como está você hoje?
Hello, what is your name?
Oi, qual é seu nome?
How old are you?
Quantos anos você tem?
This is very hard, but it's not impossible
Isto é muito difícil, mas não é impossível
Where are you from?
De onde é você?

*In Portuguese, "it's not" is flipped around *não é* or *não esta*.

*In Portuguese, in regards to the pronoun "your," there are two ways of saying it—*tua* or *seu* (male), *sua* (female). *Tua* is the informal "your." Use it when speaking to a friend or someone whom you know well, while *seu* and *sua* are the formal "your;" use them when speaking to an authority, professor, someone whom you just met, or someone to whom you show respect.

The Program

Thank you - (M)Obrigado / (F)Obrigada
For / In order to - Para
Day - Dia
Time - Tempo
No / not - Não
I am not - Eu não estou / Eu não sou
That - (M) Este, (F) Esta
It's - é / Isto é
Yesterday - Ontem
Anything - Qualquer coisa / Tudo
But - Mas
Away - Longe / Distante
Similar - Similar / Parecido
Other / Another - Outro / Um outro
Side - Lado
Until - Até
Still - Ainda / Todavia
Since - Desde
Before - Antes

Thank you Kenneth.
Obrigado Kenneth.
It's almost time
É quase tempo
I am not here, I am away.
Eu não estou aqui, estou longe.
That is a similar house to ours.
Essa casa é semelhante à nossa.
I am from the other side
Estou do outro lado
But I was here until late yesterday
Mas eu estive aqui até tarde **da** noite de ontem
Since the other day
Desde o outro dia

*This *isn't* a phrase book! The purpose of this book is *solely* to provide you with the tools to create *your own* sentences!

To be - Estar / Ser
I say / I am saying - Eu digo / Estou dizendo
I see / I am seeing - Eu vejo / Estou vendo / **To see -** Ver
I go / I am going - Eu vou / Estou indo
I want - Quero
I need - Preciso
What time is it? - Que horas são?
Without you - Sem você
Everywhere - Em todo Lugar
With - Com
My - (S)(M&F)Meu/Minha **(P)(M&F)**Meus/ Minhas
Cousin - Primo
Night - Noite
Light - Luz
Outside - Fora
That is - Isto é
Right now - Neste momento
Any - Qualquer

I am saying no
Estou dizendo não
I say no
Eu digo não
I want to see this during the day
Eu quero ver isto durante o dia
I see this everywhere
Eu vejo isso em todos os lugares
I am happy without my cousins here
Estou feliz sem os meus primos aqui
I need to be there at night
Preciso estar lá à noite
I see light outside
Eu vejo luz lá fora
What time is it right now?
Que horas são agora?

*In Portuguese, placing the pronoun "I" / *eu* before a conjugated verb isn't required. For example, "I want to use this" is *quero usar isto* instead of *eu quero usar isto*, although saying **eu** *quero usar* isn't incorrect. The same rule also applies for the pronouns "you," "he," "she," "them," and "we." Please refer to page #44.

To wait - Esperar
To sell - Vender
To use - Usar
To know - Saber
To decide - Decidir
To find - Encontrar
To look for / To search - Procurar /Buscar
To - De
Place Lugar
Easy - Fácil
Near - Perto
Between - Entre
Both - Ambos / os dois
That (conjunction) - Que

This place is easy to find
Este lugar e muito fácil de encotrar
I am saying to wait until tomorrow
Eu estou dizendo para esperar até amanhã
I want to use this
Eu quero usar isto
Where is the book?
Onde está o livro?
I need to look for you at the mall.
Eu preciso te procurar no shopping.
I need to decide between the two places
Eu preciso decidir entre os dois lugares
I am very happy to know that everything is ok
Estou muito feliz em saber que tudo está bem

*In English, an infinitive verb is always preceded by "to": "to want," "to wait," "to decide." But in Portuguese and Spanish, the *ar, er,* or *ir* at the end of the verb makes it infinitive: *querer, esperar, decidir.* Occasionally you can place a *para* preceding the infinitive verb: "to wait" / *para esperar.*

* "That" / "which" can also be used as relative pronouns. The translation in Portuguese is *que*. "I am very happy to know that everything is ok" / *estou muito feliz em saber **que** tudo está bem.*

To look - Olhar / **To buy** - Comprar
To understand - Entender / Compreender
I do / I am doing - Eu faço / Eu estou fazendo
I can / Can I - Eu Posso / Posso?
Myself - Eu mesmo / **Mine** - Meu
Them | They - (M) Eles / (F) Elas
Food - Comida / **Water** - Agua
Hotel - Hotel
Book - Livro
Problem / Problems - Problema / Problemas
Because - Porque
Like this - Asi
Of - (S)(M&F)Do/Da (P)(M&F)Dos,Das (**neuter**) De
Enough - Bastante

I like this hotel because it's near the beach
Eu gosto deste hotel porque fica perto da praia
I want to look at the view.
Eu quero olhar a vista.
I want to buy a bottle of water
Eu quero comprar uma garrafa de água
Do it like this!
Faça isso deste modo!
Both of them have enough food
Ambos deles tem bastante comida
That book is mine.
Esse livro é meu.
I need to understand the problem
Eu preciso entender o problema
I see the view of the city from the hotel
Eu vejo a vista da cidade do hotel
I can work today
Eu posso trabalhar hoje
I do what I want.
Eu faço o que eu quero.

*To learn more about the conjugation of "of," please refer to page #42.
*In the Portuguese language, certain words can connect and combine to form one. For example: *de* (of) + *eles* (them) = *deles* / *de* (of) + *este* (this) = *deste*. To learn more about these connections, please refer to Combinação e Contração on page #44.

The Program

To know - Saber
To go - Ir
To work - Trabalhar
To say - Dizer
I like - Eu gosto
Family / Parents - Família / Pais
There is / There are - Há / Aqui está / Aqui estão / São
Who - Quem
Why - Porque
Something - Algo / Alguma coisa
Ready - Pronto
Soon / quickly - Rápido / Logo

I like to be at my house with my parents
Eu gosto de estar na minha casa com meus pais
Why do I need to say something important?
Por que preciso dizer algo importante?
I am there with him
Eu estou ali com ele
I am busy, but I need to be ready soon
Eu **estou** ocupado, mas preciso estar pronto rápido
I like to work
Gosto de trabalhar
Who is there?
Quem está lá?
I want to know if they are here.
Eu quero saber se eles estão aqui.
I can go outside.
Eu posso ir lá fora.
There are seven dolls
São sete bonecas
I want to sleep
Eu quero dormir

*This *isn't* a phrase book! The purpose of this book is *solely* to provide you with the tools to create *your own* sentences!

To bring - Trazer
To Drive - Dirigir
To eat - Comer
With me - Comigo
Without me - Sem eu
How much - Quanto
Lunch - Almoço
Fast / Quickly - Rápido
Slow / Slowly - Devagar
Cold - Frio
Hot - Quente
Inside - Dentro
Instead - Em vez
Only - Somente
When - Quando
Or - Ou
Were - Erão

How much money do I need to bring with me?
Quanto dinheiro eu preciso trazer comigo?
I like bread instead of rice.
Eu gosto de pão em vez de arroz.
Only when you can
Somente quando pode
Go there without me.
Vá lá sem mim.
I need to drive the car very fast or very slowly
Eu preciso dirigir o carro muito rápido ou muito devagar
It is cold inside the library
Está frio dentro da biblioteca
I like to eat a hot meal for my lunch.
Eu gosto de comer uma refeição quente no meu almoço.

The Program

To answer - Responder
To fly - Voar
To travel - Viajar
To learn - Aprender
To swim - Nadar
To practice - Praticar
To play - Jogar
To leave - Deixar
I go to - Eu vou para
First - Primeiro
Time / Times - Vez / Vezes
Like (*preposition*) **-** Como
How - Como
Many / A lot - Muito / Muitas

I need to answer many questions
Eu preciso responder muitas perguntas
I want to fly today
Eu quero voar hoje
I need to learn how to swim at the pool
Eu preciso aprender como nadar na piscina
I want to learn how to play better tennis.
Eu quero aprender a jogar tênis melhor.
Everything is about the money.
Tudo é sobre o dinheiro.
I want to leave my dog at home.
Eu quero deixar meu cachorro em casa.
I want to travel the world.
Eu quero viajar pelo mundo.
Since the first time
Desde a primeira vez
The children are yours
As crianças são tuas

*ature *Pelo mundo* literally means "throughout the world."

*With the knowledge you've gained so far, now try to create your own sentences!

To visit - Visitar
To walk - Caminhar / Andar
To give - Dar
To meet - Conhecer
Someone - Alguém
Us - Nós
Mom / Mother - Mamãe / Mãe
Nothing / Anything - Nada
Nobody / anyone - Ninguém
Against - Contra
Which - Qual
Just - Apenas
Around - Ao redor / em volta
Towards – Para / a traves
Than - Que

Something is better than nothing
Alguma coisa é melhor que nada
I am against him
Eu estou contra ele
We go to visit my family each week
Vamos visitar minha familia cada semana
I need to give you something
Eu preciso te dar algo
Do you want to meet someone?
Você quer conhecer alguém?
I am here on Wednesdays as well
Eu estou aqui às quartas-feiras também
You do this everyday?
Você faz isso todos os dias?
You need to walk around the school.
Você precisa andar pela escola.

Te is a direct and indirect object pronoun, the person who is actually affected by the action that is being carried out. But *te* comes before the verb. For example, "I love you" / *eu te amo* or "to give you" / *te dar*.

The Program

To show - Mostrar
To prepare - Preperar
To borrow - Emprestar
To look like - Parecer
To want - Querer
To stay - Ficar
To continue - Continuar
I have / I must - Eu tenho / Eu devo
I am not going - Eu não vou
Don't / Doesn't - Não
Friend - Amigo
Grandfather - Avô
Way (road) - Caminho
Way (method) - Maneira
That's why - Por isso

Do you want to look like Arnold?
Você quer parecer como Arnold?
I want to borrow this book for my grandfather
Eu quero emprestar este livro do meu avô
I want to drive and to continue on this way to my house
Eu quero dirigir para continuar neste caminho para minha casa
I want to stay in São Paulo because I have a friend there
Eu tenho um amigo em São Paulo, por isso eu quero estar lá
I am not going to see anyone here
Eu não vou ver ninguém aqui
I need to show you how to prepare breakfast
Eu preciso te mostrar como preparar o café da manhã
Why don't you have the book?
Por que você não tem o livro?
That is incorrect, I don't need the car today
Isto nao e certo, eu não preciso do carro hoje.

To remember - Lembrar
To think - Pensar
To do - Fazer
To come - Vir
To hear - Escutar
Your - (S)(M)Teu, (F)Tua / (P)(M)Teus, (F)Tuas
Grandmother - Avó
Dark / darkness - Escuro / Escuridão
Number - Número
Five - Cinco
Hour - Hora
Minute / minutes - Minuto / Minutos
A second - Um segundo
Moment - Momento
Last - (M)Último /**(F)**Última
More - Mais
About - Sobre

You need to remember your number
Você precisa lembrar teu número
This is the last hour of darkness
Esta é a última hora da escuridão
I want to come with you.
Eu quero ir com você.
I can hear my grandmother speaking Portuguese.
Eu posso ouvir minha avó falando português.
I need to think about this more.
Eu preciso pensar mais sobre isso.
From here until there, it's just five minutes
Daqui até ali, é apenas cinco minutos.

The Program

To leave - Sair
To take - Tomar
To try - Tentar
To rent - Alugar
To turn off - Apagar
To ask - Pedir
To stop - Parar
Without her - Sem ela
We are - Estamos / Somos
Brazil - Brasil
Again - Outra vez / de novo
Permission - Permissão

He needs to go to rent a house at the beach
Ele precisa ir e alugar uma casa na praia
I want to take the test without her
Eu quero tomar um teste sem ela
We are here a long time
Nós estamos aqui por muito tempo
I need to turn off the lights early
Eu preciso desligar as luzes cedo
We want to stop here
Nós queremos parar aqui
We are from Brazil.
Nós somos do Brasil.
Your doctor is in the same building.
O seu médico está no mesmo prédio.
In order to leave you have to ask permission.
Para sair, você precisa pedir permissão.

To open - Abrir
To buy - Comprar
To pay - Pagar
To clean - Limpar
To hope - Esperar
To live - Viver
To return - Regressar
Without - Sem
Door - Porta
Sister - Irmã
Nice to meet you - Prazer em conhecer lo
Name - Nome
Last name - Sobrenome
Enough - Suficiente

I need to open the door for my sister
Eu preciso abrir a porta para minha irmã
I need to buy something
Eu preciso comprar alguma coisa
I want to meet your brothers.
Eu quero conhecer seus irmãos.
Nice to meet you, what is your name and your last name?
Prazer em conhecer lo, qual é o seu nome e, o seu sobrenome?
We can hope for a better future.
Podemos esperar um futuro melhor.
It is impossible to live without problems.
É impossível viver sem problemas.
I want to return to the United States.
Eu quero voltar para os Estados Unidos.
Why are you sad right now?
Porque você està triste em neste momento?
Our house is on the mountain.
Nossa casa fica na montanha.

*This *isn't* a phrase book! The purpose of this book is *solely* to provide you with the tools to create *your own* sentences!

The Program

To happen - Ocorrer / acontecer
To order - Ordenar
To drink - Beber
To begin / to start - Começar
To finish - Terminar
To help - Ajudar
To smoke - Fumar
To love - Amar
To talk / to speak - Falar
Excuse me - Desculpa
Child - Criança
Woman - Mulher

This needs to happen today
Isto precisa acontecer hoje
Excuse me, my child is here as well
Desculpe, minha criança está aqui também
I want to order a soup.
Eu quero pedir uma sopa.
We want to start the class soon.
Queremos começar a aula em breve.
In order to finish at three o'clock this afternoon, I need to finish soon
Para terminar às três horas da tarde, preciso terminar em breve
I want to learn how to speak perfect Portuguese
Quero aprender a falar português perfeito
I don't want to smoke again
Eu não quero fumar outra vez
I want to help
Eu quero ajudar
I love you
Eu te amo
I see you
Eu te vejo
I need you
Eu preciso de ti

*In Portuguese, "child" is *criança*, "son" is *filho*, and "daughter" is *filha*.

To read - Ler
To write - Escrever
To teach - Ensinar
To close - Fechar
To turn on - Acender / Ligar
To prefer - Preferir
To choose – Escolher
To put - Por / colocar
I talk / I speak - Eu Falo
Sun - Sol
Month - Mês
Less - Menos
Exact - (**M**)Exato / (**F**)exata

II need this book to learn how to read and write in Portuguese
Preciso deste livro para aprender a lere e escrever em português
I want to teach English in Brazil
Quero ensinar em inglês no brasil
I want turn on the lights and close the door.
Quero acender as luzes e fechar a porta.
I want to pay less than you.
Eu quero pagar menos do que você.
I prefer to put this here.
Eu prefiro colocar isso aqui.
I speak with the boy and the girl in Spanish and Portuguese
Eu falo com o menino e a menina em espanhol e português
There is sun outside today
Há sol lá fora hoje
Is it possible to know the exact date?
É possível saber a data exata?

*In English, adjectives usually precede the verb. In Portuguese, it's usually the opposite (i.e., "exact date" / *data exata* or "blue car" / *carro azul*).

*With the knowledge you've gained so far, now try to create your own sentences!

The Program

To exchange - Trocar / Cambiar
To call - Chamar
To sit - Sentar
To change - Trocar
To follow - Seguir
Him / Her - Lo /La
Brother - Irmão / **Dad** - Papai
Together - Juntos
Of course - Claro
Welcome - Bemvindo
Years - Anos
Sky - Céu
Up - Encima / **Down** - Abaixo
Sorry - Desculpe
Big - Grande
New - Novo
Never - Jamais / Nunca
During - Durante

I never want to exchange this money at the bank
Eu nunca quero trocar este dinheiro no banco
I want to call my brother and my dad today
Eu quero chamar meu irmão e meu papai hoje
Of course I can come to the theater, and I want to sit together with you and your sister
Claro eu posso vir a teatro, e eu quero sentar junto contigo e com tua irmã
If you look under the table, you can see the new rug.
Se você olhar embaixo da mesa, poderá ver o novo tapete
I can see the sky from the window
Eu posso ver o céu da janela
I am sorry.
Sinto muito.
The dog wants to follow me to the store.
O cachorro quer me seguir até a loja.

*In Portuguese, *lo* and *la* are used as direct masculine, feminine, and neuter object pronouns, meaning "him," "her," or "it."
* to see him / *vê-lo*
* to follow her / *sigu-la*
The *r* at the end of the infinitive verb is removed.

To allow - Permitir / deixar
To believe - Crer
To enter - Entrar
To receive - Receber
To move - Mover / Mudar
To promise - Prometer
To recognize - Reconhecer
Morning - Manhã
Good night - Boa noite
Good afternoon - Boa tarde
People - Pessoas
Except - Exceto
Free - Gratis
Far - Distante
Different - Diferente
Throughout - Em todo
Through - Atravez

I need to allow him to go with us.
Eu preciso permitir que ele vá conosco.
He is a different man now.
Ele é um homem diferente agora.
I believe everything except for this
Eu acredito em tudo exceto isto
Come here quickly.
Venha aqui rapidamente.
I must promise to say good night to my parents each night
Eu preciso prometer de dizer boa noite a meu pais cada noite.
I can't recognize him.
Eu não consigo reconhecê-lo.
I need to move your cat to a different chair
Eu preciso mudar seu gato para uma outra cadeira
They want to enter the competition and receive a free book
Eles querem entrar na competiçao e receber um livro gratis
I see the sun throughout the morning from the kitchen
Eu vejo o sol em toda manhã pelo cozinha
I go into the house from the front entrance and not through the yard.
Entro na casa pela entrada da frente e não pelo quintal.

The Program

To wish - Desejar
To get - Conseguir
To forget - Esquecer
To feel - Sentir
To like - Gostar
See you soon / Goodbye - Vejo você logo / Tchau
Everybody - Todos
Restaurant - Restaurante
Bathroom - Banheiro
Person - Pessoa
Bad - Mal / mau
Great - Grande
Next - Próximo
In front - Em frente
Behind - Atras
Well - Bem
Although - Embora

I don't want to wish you anything bad
Eu não quero desejar a você nada de mal
I must forget everybody from my past.
Devo esquecer todos do meu passado.
I am next to the person behind you
Eu estou próximo da pessoa atrás de você
To feel well I must take vitamins
Para me sentir bem, devo tomar vitaminas
There is a great person in front of me
Aqui esta uma pessoa grande na minha frente
Goodbye my friend.
Adeus meu amigo.
Which is the best restaurant in the area?
Qual é o melhor restaurante da região?
I can feel the heat.
Eu posso sentir o calor.
I need to repair a part of the cabinet of the bathroom.
Eu preciso consertar uma parte do armário do banheiro.
She has to get a car before the next year
Ela tem que conseguir um carro antes do próximo ano
I like the house, but it is very small
Eu gosto desta casa, mas este muito pequena

To remove - Remover / Retirar
To sleep - Dormir
To lift - Levantar / **To hold** - Segurar
To check - Revisar
Include / Including - Incluir / Incluindo
Belong - Pertencer
Week - Semana
Beautiful - **(M)**Lindo / **(F)**Linda
Please - Por favor
Price - Preço
Small - Pequeno
Real - Real / Verdade
Size - Tamanho
Even though - Mesmo que
So - Então

She wants to remove this door please
Por favor, ela quer remover esta porta
This doesn't belong here, I need to check again
Isto não pertencer aqui, preciso revisar outra vez
This week the weather was very beautiful
Esta semana, o tempo estava muito bonito
Is that a real diamond?
Isso é um diamante de verdade?
We need to check the size of the house
Eu preciso revisar o tamanho desta casa
I want to lift this.
Eu quero levantar isso.
The sun is high in the sky.
O sol está alto no céu.
Can you please hold my hand?
Você pode por favor segurar minha mão?
Can you please put the wood in the fire?
Você pode por favor colocar a lenha no fogo?
I can pay this although the price is expensive
Eu posso pagar isto, embora o preço e caro
Including everything, is this price correct?
Incluindo tudo, este preço está correto
I want to go to sleep
Eu quero ir dormir

Building Bridges

In Building Bridges, we take six conjugated verbs that have been selected after studies I have conducted for several months in order to determine which verbs are most commonly conjugated, and which are then automatically followed by an infinitive verb. For example, once you know how to say, "I need," "I want," "I can," and "I like," you will be able to connect words and say almost anything you want more correctly and understandably. The following three pages contain these six conjugated verbs in first, second, third, fourth, and fifth person, as well as some sample sentences. Please master the entire program up until *here* prior to venturing onto this section.

I want - Quero
I need - Preciso
I can - Posso
I like - Gosto
I go - Vou
I have / I must – Tenho

I want to go to my house
Eu quero ir a minha casa
I can go with you to the bus station
Eu posso ir contigo para a estação de ônibus
I need to leave the museum.
Eu preciso sair do museu.
I like to eat oranges.
Eu gosto de comer laranjas.
I am going to teach a class
Eu vou ensinar uma classe
I have to speak to my teacher
Tenho que falar com meu professor

Please master *every* single page up until here prior to attempting the following pages!

You want / do you want? - Você quer
He wants / does he want? - Ele quer
She wants / does she want? - Ela quer
We want / do we want? - Nós queremos
They want / do they want? - Eles/elas querem
You (plural) want? - Vocês querem

You need / do you need? - Você precisa
He needs / does he need? - Ele precisa
She needs / does she need? - Ela precisa
We want / do we want? - Nós precisamos
They need / do they need? - Eles/elas precisam
You (plural) need? - Vocês precisam

You can / can you? - Você pode
He can / can he? - Ele pode
She can / can she? - Ela pode
We can / can we? - Nós podemos
They can / can they? - Eles/elas Podem
You (plural) can? - Vocês podem

You like / do you like? - Você gosta
He likes / does he like? - Ele gosta
She like / does she like? - Ela gosta
We like / do we like? - Nós gostamos
They like / do they like? - Eles/elas gostam
You (plural) like? - Vocês gostam

You go / do you go? - Você vai
He goes / does he go? - Ele vai
She goes / does she go? - Ela vai
We go / do we go? - Nós vamos
They go / do they go? - Eles/elas vão
You (plural) go? - Vocês vão

You have / do you have? - Você tem
He has / does he have? - Ele tem
She has / does she have? - Ela tem
We have / do we have? - Nós temos
They have / do they have? - Eles/elas têm
You (plural) have? - Vocês têm?

Building Bridges

Do you want to go?
Você quer ir?

Does he want to fly?
Ele quer voar?

We want to swim
Queremos nadar

Do they want to run?
Querem correr

Do you need to clean?
Você precisa limpar?

She needs to sing a song
Ela precisa cantar um canção

We need to travel
Precisamos viajar

They don't need to fight
Eles não precisam lutar

You (plural) need to save your money.
Vocês (plural) precisam economizar seu dinheiro.

Can you hear me?
Pode me escuctar?

He can dance very well
Pode dançar muito bem

We can go out tonight
Podemos sair esta noite

The fireman can break the door during an emergency.
O bombeiro pode quebrar a porta durante uma emergência.

Do you like to eat here?
Gosta de comer aqui?

He likes to spend time here
Gosta de passar tempo aqui

We like to fix the house
Gostamos de arrumar a casa

They like to cook
Eles gostam de cozinhar

You (plural) like to play soccer.
Vocês (plural) gostam de jogar futebol.

Do you go to school today?
Você vai à escola hoje

He goes fishing
Ele vai pescar

We are going to relax
Vamos relaxer

They go out to eat at a restaurant everyday.
Eles saem para comer em um restaurante todos os dias.

Do you go to the movies on weekends?
Você vai ao cinema nos fins de semana?

Do you have money?
Você tem dinheiro?

She has to look outside
Ela tem que olhar para fora

We have to sign our names
Temos que assinar os nossos nomes

They have to send the letter
Eles tem que mandar/enviar a carta

You (plural) have to stand in line.
Vocês (plural) têm que ficar na fila.

---

*Whenever referring to a group in which you have all female individuals, you refer to that group as *elas*. Mixed male and female individuals refer to them as *eles*.

If you enjoyed this book, then check out "Part 2" which is available for sale on all online book retail platforms.

Basic Grammatical Requirements of the Portuguese Language

Feminine and Masculine & Plural and Singular

In the Portuguese language, there are plural and singular words, as well as masculine and feminine words. For example, the article "the," for Portuguese words ending with an *a, e,* and *i,* will usually be deemed to be feminine, the article will usually be *a*. Nouns ending with an *o* will generally be masculine, and the article will usually be *o*. The article "the" in plural form is *os* for the masculine form, and *as* for the feminine form. "The boy" is *o (the) menino (boy)*. "The girl" is *a menina*, "the boys" is *os meninos*, and "the girls" is *as meninas*.

The conjugation of the article "a" (*um* and *uma*) is determined by masculine and feminine form: "a car" / *um carro* or "a house" / *uma casa*.

The conjugation for "this" (*esta, este, estes,* and *estas*) and "that" (*esse, essa, esses,* and *essas*). This, *este* is masculine, *este livro* ("this book"). Feminine is *esta,* for example, *esta casa* ("this house"). *Estes livros* ("these books") and *estas casas* ("these houses") are the plural forms. "That," *esse,* is masculine, *esse livro* ("that book"). Feminine is *essa, essa cadeira* ("that chair"). In plural, that is *esses livros* (these books) and *essas cadeiras* ("these chairs").

"Of" has singular and plural forms as well: *do* and *dos*.

Isso and *isto* are neuter pronouns, meaning they don't have a gender. They usually refer to an idea or an unknown object that isn't specifically named. For example, "that" is *isto*.
* *isto é* / "that is"
* *por isso* / "because of that"

"This" is *isto*.
* *isto esta bom* / "this is good"
* *o que é isto?* / "what is this?"

In regards to "my," singular and plural form exists as well as feminine and masculine. *Meu* is masculine, *minha* is feminine, *meus* is masculine plural, and *minhas* is feminine plural.
* "my chair" / *minha cadeira*
* "my chairs" / *minhas cadeiras*
* "my money" / *meu dinheiro*
* "my papers" / *meus papéis*

With regard to "your," *teu* (masculine) and *tua* (feminine), plural *teus* and *tuas*. Example in masculine and feminine singular:
* *teu carro* / "your car"
* *your house* / "tua casa"

The plural *teus carros* and *tuas casas*.

Temporary and Permanent

The different forms of "is" are *é* and *está*. When referring to a permanent condition, for example, "she is a girl" / *ela é uma menina,* you use *é*. For temporary positions, "the girl is doing well today" / *a menina está muito bem hoje,* you use *está*.

"You are" / "are you" could mean *estas,* and it could also mean *tu eres*. An example of temporary position is "How are you today?" / *"Como você está?"* as well as "you are here" / *está aqui*.

Another example of permanent position is "are you Mexican?" / *você é Mexicano?* in addition to "You are a man!" / *você é um homem!*

* **"I am"**—**estou and eu sou.** *Eu sou* refers to a permanent condition: "I am Italian" / *eu sou Italiano.* Temporary condition would be "I am at the mall" / *estou no mall.*

* **"We are"**—**somos (permanent) and estamos (temporary).** *Nós somos brasileiros* / "we are Brazilian" and *nós estamos no parque* / "we are at the park."

* **"Are"**—**são (permanent) and estão (temporary).** *Eles são Chilenos* / "they are Chileans" and *eles estão no carro* / "they are in the car."

Synonyms and Antonyms

There are three ways of describing time.

Vez / vezes—"first time" / *primeira vez* or "three times" / *três vezes*

Tempo—"during the time of the dinosaurs" / *durante o tempo dos dinossauros*

Hora—"What time is it?" / *Que hora são?*

Que has four definitions.

"What"—*O que é isso?* / "What is this?"

"Than"—*Eu estou melhor que você* / "I am better than you"

"That"—"I want to say that I am near the house" / *eu quero dizer que estou perto da casa*

"I must" / "I have to"—*Tenho que.* The verb *ter,* "to have," whether it's in conjugated or infinitive form, if it's followed by another verb, then *que* must always follow.

For example: I have to swim now, *tenho que nadar agora.*

Deixar has two definitions.

"To leave"—*Eu quero deixar isto aqui* / "I want to leave this here." *Deixar* is "to leave" something, but when saying "to leave" as in "going," it's *sair*, for example, "I want to leave now" / *quero sair agora.*

"To allow"—*Deixar* could also mean to "allow."

There are two ways of describing "so."

"So"—*então*. Using it to replace "then." "So I need to know." / *Então preciso saber.*

"So"—*tão. Isso é tão distante.* / "This is so far."

Verb Conjugation in First Person

"I" / *Eu* before a conjugated verb isn't required. For example, *Eu preciso saber a data* / "I need to know the date" can be said *Preciso saber a data,* because *preciso* already means "I need," in conjugated form. Although saying *Eu* isn't incorrect! The same can also be said with *você / tu; ele / ela; nós; eles / elas*, in which they aren't required to be placed prior to the conjugated verb, but if they are, then it isn't wrong.

Combinação e contração

In Portuguese, certain words can connect, creating one syllable. For example, the article "the," in masculine form *o*, feminine form *a*:

*In(**em**)+the(**o**)=**no**, in the car, **no** carro*

***em+a=na**, in the house, **na** casa*

*In(**em**) and this(**essa**), **em+essa; nessa;** In this house, **nessa** casa*

*In this car; **em+esse; nesse** carro*

***em+este = neste; neste** carro*

***em+esta = nesta** casa*

In(em) his(ele) = *nele; in his car,* **nele** *carro*

In(em) her(ela) = *nela; in her house,* **nela** *casa*

Our house, **Nossa** *casa / Our car,* **Nosso** *carro*

His car, **de+ele** = *carro* **dele** */ her car, carro* **dela**

Their car, carro **deles** */ (fem) their car / carro* **delas**

Of and *this* can connect as well creating one syllable,

de+isso; *I need this, eu preciso* **disso**

de+esse; *from this side,* **desse** *lado*

de+esses; *these men,* **desses** *homes*

de+essas; *these women,* **dessas** *mulheres*

de+isso = **disto**

de+aqui = **daqui**

de+onde = **donde**

de+outro = **doutro**

Reading and Pronunciation

Ã can be pronounced as either "uh" or "un" however it must be nasalized. *Cão* pronounced as sun-o.

Ç is pronounced like "s," whenever it precedes *a, o,* or *u*. *Criança* is pronounced as "criansa."

D is pronounced as "dj" whenever preceding an *i* or an *e*. *Tarde* is pronounced as "tardje." *Dia* is pronounced as "gia."

H is silent except when followed by an *n*.

L is pronounced as "ee-oo" whenever it follows an *a* or *i*. *Brasil* is pronounced as "Bra-zee-oo."

M is pronounced as a soft "m" whenever it's the last letter of a word. One trick for pronunciation is saying it without closing your lips.

R is pronounced as an "h" if it's the first letter of the word. *Roberto* is "Hoberto." Whenever *r* is the last letter of a word, then it's pronounced very softly.

S is pronounced like a "z" whenever it's between vowels or when it's at the end of the word. *Português* is pronounced as "Portuguêz."

T is pronounced as "tchi" whenever preceding an *e* or an *i*. *Contigo* is pronounced as "contchigo."

U is pronounced like "oo."

W is pronounced like a "v." *William* is pronounced as "Villiam."

X is usually pronounced as "ch" whenever preceding a vowel. *Deixar* is pronounced as "deis har." Whenever preceding a consonant, *X* is usually pronounced as "s." *Exterior* is pronounced as "esterior." When between vowels, *X* is usually pronounced as "ks." *Fixo* is "fikso." For words that begin in *ex* or *hex*, followed by a vowel, the *x* is pronounced like a *z*. *Hexágono* is "hezágono." But in Portuguese, *x* is one of those letters where there are no set rules for its pronunciation!

Z is pronounced as a "ss" whenever it's at the end of a word. *Alvarez* is pronounced as "Alvaress."

Diphthongs
ai - is pronounced like the *ie* in *pie*
ão – ("a with a tilde and o") is pronounced like the *ow* in *clown*
au - is pronounced like the *ow* in *now*
ei - is pronounced like the *ay* in *pay*
eu - is pronounced as *ay-oo* like the *ay* in *hay* + the *oo* in *boot*
ho - is pronounced like a soft *o*
ia - is pronounced *ee-ah* like the *ee* in *feet* + the *a* in *father*
ie - is pronounced like the *e* in *yes*
io - is pronounced *ee-oh*
iu - is pronounced *ee-oo* like the *ee* in *meet* + the *oo* in *loot*
oi - is pronounced "closed" like the *oy* in *toy*
ou - is pronounced like the *ow* in *glow*
õ - is pronounced nasalized
ua - is pronounced like the *oo-ah* in *watch* minus the *w* sound
ue - is pronounced *oo-eh* like the *oo* in *loot* and the *ay* in *day*
ui - is pronounced like *oo-ee* the *oo* in *loot* and the *ee* in *meet*
uo - is pronounced like the *uo* in *quota*

Diagraphs
lh - is pronounced like *lli* in *alligator*
nh - is pronounced like *ni* in *minion*; or like *mañana* in Spanish
rr - pronounced like *h as in english*, *terra* will be pronounced *teh-ha*

Accents
Á – ("A with an acute accent") is pronounced like the *y* in *fly*, when at the end of the word pronounced like *a* in *another*
À – ("A with a grave accent") is pronounced like the *a* in *another*
Â – ("A with a circumflex accent") is pronounced like a long *a*
É – (E with an acute accent) is pronounced like the *a* in *many*
Ê – (E with a circumflex accent") pronounced like a long *e*
Ì – (I with an acute accent) is pronounced like the *e* in embrace
Ô – ("O with a circumflex accnet") is pronounced like a long *o*
Ó – (O with an acute accent) is pronounced like *oy*. However when it's the last letter of word then it's like *u* in *jump*
Ú – (U with an acute accent or U with circumflex accent) is pronounced like the *oo* in *loot*.

Other Useful Tools in the Portuguese Language

Days of the Week - Días de la semana
Sunday - Domingo
Monday - Segunda-feira
Tuesday - Terça-feira
Wednesday - Quarta-feira
Thursday - Quinta-feira
Friday - Sexta-feira
Saturday - Sábado

Seasons
Spring - Primavera / **Summer -** Verão
Autumn - Outono / **Winter -** Inverno

Colors
Black - Preto
White - Branco
Gray - Cinza
Red - Vermelho
Blue - Azul
Yellow - Amarelo
Green - Verde
Orange - Laranja
Purple - Roxo
Brown - Marrom

Numbers
One - Um
Two - Dois
Three - Três
Four - Quatro
Five - Cinco
Six - Sies
Seven - Sete
Eight - Oito
Nine - Nove
Ten - Dez

Cardinal Directions
North - Norte / **South -** Sul
East - Leste / **West –** Oeste

Congratulations! Now You Are on Your Own!

If you merely absorb the required three hundred and fifty words in this book, you will then have acquired the basis to become conversational in Portuguese! After memorizing these three hundred and fifty words, this conversational foundational basis that you have just gained will trigger your ability to make improvements in conversational fluency at an amazing speed! However, in order to engage in quick and easy conversational communication, you need a special type of basics, and this book will provide you with just that.

Unlike the foreign language learning systems presently used in schools and universities, along with books and programs that are available on the market today, that focus on *everything* but being conversational, *this* method's sole focus is on becoming conversational in Portuguese as well as any other language. Once you have successfully mastered the required words in this book, there are two techniques that if combined with these essential words, can further enhance your skills and will result in you improving your proficiency tenfold. *However*, these two techniques will only succeed *if* you have completely and successfully absorbed the three hundred and fifty words. *After* you establish the basis for fluent communications by memorizing these words, you can enhance your conversational abilities even more if you use the following two techniques.

The first step is to attend a Portuguese language class that will enable you to sharpen your grammar. You will gain additional vocabulary and learn past and present tenses, and if you apply these skills that you learn in the class, together with the three hundred and fifty words that you have previously memorized, you will be improving your conversational skills tenfold. You will notice that, conversationally, you will succeed at a much higher rate than any of your classmates. A simple second technique is to choose Portuguese subtitles while watching a movie. If you have successfully mastered and grasped these three hundred and fifty words, then the combination of the two—those words along with the subtitles—will aid you considerably in putting all the grammar into perspective, and again, conversationally, you will improve tenfold.

Once you have established a basis of quick and easy conversation in Portuguese with those words that you just attained, every additional word or grammar rule you pick up from there on will be gravy. And these additional words or grammar rules can be combined with the three hundred and fifty words, enriching your conversational abilities even more. Basically, after the research and studies I've conducted with my method over the years, I came to the conclusion that in order to become conversational, you first must learn the words and *then* learn the grammar.

The Portuguese language is compatible with the mirror translation technique. Likewise, with *this* language, you can use this mirror translation technique in order to become conversational, enabling you to communicate even more effortlessly. Mirror translation is the method of translating a phrase or sentence, word for word from English to Portuguese, by using these imperative words that you have acquired through this program (such as the sentences I used in this book). Latin languages, Middle Eastern languages, and Slavic languages, along with a few others, are also compatible with the mirror translation technique. Though you won't be speaking perfectly proper and precise Portuguese, you will still be fully understood and, conversation-wise, be able to get by just fine.

Conclusion

Congratulations! You have completed all the tools needed to master the Portuguese language, and I hope that this has been a valuable learning experience. Now you have sufficient communication skills to be confident enough to embark on a visit to Brazil, impress your friends, and boost your resume so *good luck.*

This program is available in other languages as well, and it is my fervent hope that my language learning programs will be used for good, enabling people from all corners of the globe and from all cultures and religions to be able to communicate harmoniously. After memorizing the required three hundred and fifty words, please perform a daily five-minute exercise by creating sentences in your head using these words. This simple exercise will help you grasp conversational communications even more effectively. Also, once you memorize the vocabulary on each page, follow it by using a notecard to cover the words you have just memorized and test yourself and follow *that* by going back and using this same notecard technique on the pages you studied during the previous days. This repetition technique will assist you in mastering these words in order to provide you with the tools to create your own sentences.

Every day, use this notecard technique on the words that you have just studied.

Everything in life has a catch. The catch here is just consistency. If you just open the book, and after the first few pages of studying the program, you put it down, then you will not gain anything. However, if you consistently dedicate a half hour daily to studying, as well as reviewing what you have learned from previous days, then you will quickly realize why this method is the most effective technique ever created to become conversational in a foreign language. My technique works! For anyone who doubts this technique, all I can say is that it has worked for me and hundreds of others.

.

NOTE FROM THE AUTHOR

Thank you for your interest in my work. I encourage you to share your overall experience of this book by posting a review. Your review can make a difference! Please feel free to describe how you benefited from my method or provide creative feedback on how I can improve this program. I am constantly seeking ways to enhance the quality of this product, based on personal testimonials and suggestions from individuals like you.

Thanks and best of luck,
Yatir Nitzany

www.ingramcontent.com/pod-product-compliance
Lightning Source LLC
Chambersburg PA
CBHW052106110526
44591CB00013B/2375